Seven Schemes of Satan

By
Kim Dean May

Seven Schemes of Satan
by Kim Dean May

Printed in the United States of America

ISBN 9781619969063

Unless otherwise indicated, Bible quotations are taken from the New International Version. Copyright © 1973, 1978, 1984 by International Bible Society.

While every attempt has been made to ensure that the information provided in this book stands as accurate, the author is not responsible for any errors or omissions, or for any results obtained from the use of this information. The information in this book should not be used as a substitute for consultation with appropriate professionals such as ministers, therapists, or physicians.

Cover photo and design by Luke Davis

www.xulonpress.com

Contents

Dedication. vii

Introduction ix

Chapter 1   Invalidation 11

Chapter 2   Isolation 20

Chapter 3   Indulgence. 30

Chapter 4   Idealism 40

Chapter 5   Ignorance. 50

Chapter 6   Imitation 60

Chapter 7   Insecurity. 73

Summary. 83

Endnotes 89

Dedication

In honor of the one and only true God,
Jesus Christ, who appeared on earth to
destroy the work of the devil
(1 John 3:8).

Dedication

Introduction

*J*esus prayed, *"Sanctify them by the truth; your word is truth."* (John 17:17) Followers of Christ are sanctified, set apart as holy and distinct from the world's preoccupation with sin, by the power of God's truth. His word, the Bible, comprises the truth, what is right and good in contrast to what is wrong and evil. This divine truth envelopes both resistant and triumphant power, which conquers temptations from Satan, the devil, the father of lies.

Though Satan cleverly attempts to deceive, the application of scripture liberates us from misbeliefs, thoughts presented by Satan which contain partial truth or complete falsehood. By the written word of God, then, we stay in alignment with the Lord's will—His way, His truth and His life purposed for us in Christ. It's good news! Satan's schemes can't distract, detour, discourage or defeat us as we walk in the light of God's word as His sanctified children.

The following chapters will unveil seven of the devil's strategies, how he endeavors to lure us away from devotion to Christ and destroy our spiritual vitality. Take heed! The answers to our enemy's madness also lie within these pages, pragmatic, profound and powerful. *"For the word of God is living and active. Sharper than any double-edged sword, it penetrates even to dividing soul and spirit, joints and marrow; it judges the thoughts and attitudes of the heart."* (Hebrews 4:12)

Chapter 1

Invalidation

"It is difficult to make a man miserable while he feels...kindred to the great God who made him."
Abraham Lincoln

I could hardly believe my ears when I heard a high school basketball team defeated their opponent by scoring 100 points in the first half, and then cruised to victory with a record-setting performance of points scored in one game. Although the victors fell shy of 200, their coach used his five best players to impose a full-court press to start the second half ... with the score 100 to 12! Were they scared of the most miraculous comeback in the history of sports? Certainly not. This wasn't a tactic of fear, rather one of power. No concern of how their opponent felt, no respect for the other school, no caring for anyone but their objective to intimidate, maybe even invalidate. And for what purpose? Supposedly to prepare for the playoffs! But let's get real here. The primary goal and likely the only result of such an athletic slaughter was pride, selfishness exalting its triune god of me, myself, and I.

To invalidate is to devalue a person's sense of worth, leaving them feeling weak, inferior, or useless. This depicts the first scheme of Satan who not only wants to defeat Christians, but destroy them by executing a heartless strategy ... no mercy! This is why the apostle Peter wrote, *"Be self-controlled and alert. Your enemy the devil prowls around like a roaring lion looking for someone to devour."* (1 Peter 5:8) Yes, as Christ-followers we face an opponent who longs to swallow up our spiritual life like a vicious lion devouring its prey. He attempts this not by outscoring us (external), but by outwitting us (internal). It is not a game. This is a battle. The apostle Paul referred to our enemy's tactic: *"The reason I wrote you was to see if you would stand the test and be obedient in everything ... in order that Satan might not outwit us. For we were not unaware of his schemes."* (2 Corinthians 2:9, 11)

The schemes of Satan start out as thoughts. These thoughts try to outwit us, to deceive with lies that can pull us away from truth found ultimately in Jesus. So our spirituality directly relates to what thoughts we accept and live by, day to day, even moment to moment. Psychologists suggest the average person generates forty to fifty thousand thoughts daily, 70% of which are negative or untrue. Exceptionally focused people, like professional athletes or medical doctors, can potentially reduce their thoughts (often called self-talk) to twenty thousand per day with less than 50% negative in nature.[1] No wonder 1 Peter 5:8 tells us to be self-controlled and alert! We receive a myriad of input filtering into the battleground of our mind, some trying to outwit us and cause invalidation, a sense of weakness, inferiority, or uselessness.

This scheme trapped my friend, Antonio, a pastor with whom I worked on staff at a large church. He was blessed with a wonderful wife and 4 children. Antonio got along quite well with co-workers, church members, and people in general. However, I didn't see the closeness expected between this spiritual leader and his spouse. Instead of nurturing their marital relationship he spent inordinate amounts of time working at the church office. I never anticipated what was lurking under the surface, his secret sin of homosexual obsession. In fact, Antonio had been setting up sexual rendezvous with men late at night in public locations like gas stations. Found out, he was immediately fired. Then he abandoned his wife and kids for a lifestyle of homosexual encounters. Last I heard, he had moved numerous times around the country, taking various jobs to stay afloat financially, a spiritual vagabond devoured by the enemy.

The spiritual casualty of my friend did not occur in a day or a week. Over the course of time the devil prowled around like a roaring lion, instilling dark thoughts in his mind to entice him on a wayward search for satisfaction. The futile journey cost more than imaginable—the destruction of his marriage, the failure of his fatherhood, the end of his career, the loss of his friends, his church, his house, his everything. Antonio succumbed to invalidation.

After following Jesus for many years, he neglected the self-control and alertness of 1 Peter 5:8, qualities which refer to sobriety. In other words, he did not reject lies of Satan that intoxicated him with deceit and left him feeling weak, inferior, and useless.

Thoughts come and go of course. And God gives us the ability to choose which ones we latch onto, whether positive or negative, true or untrue, life-giving or life-destroying. Like my old friend Antonio, if we decide to believe false and misleading messages we can cause unbridled damage to ourselves and others. Thankfully, Jesus demonstrates how to cast aside untrue thoughts which form temptations: After fasting forty days, Satan tempted Him, *"If you are the Son of God, tell these stones to become bread." Jesus answered, "It is written: 'Man does not live on bread alone, but on every word that comes from the mouth of God.'"* (Matthew 4:3-4)

Rejecting the enemy's suggestion, along with others in this passage, Jesus cut off the schemes of Satan! Certainly Jesus was hungry and beyond hungry after fasting so long. But He remained devoted to the Father's will, refusing to take a short-cut to meet his physical need. He replaced the idea of turning stones into bread with the truth that God is the source of all we need and His word is the transcendent life-line. Therefore, Jesus did not buy into the false message that food, something earthly and temporal, could sustain one in the will of God

At this point Jesus had not begun His ministry of preaching the truth about God or healing the sick to demonstrate the presence of God or even calling

His first disciple to follow God. The Lord's refusal to embrace temptation, then, took on increasing significance. Have you realized the profound nature of this moment? In the attempt to seduce Jesus into performing a miracle outside the plan of God and thus begin serving His own wants and needs (previous to the initial step of fulfilling His assignment from heaven), Satan aspired to prevent Christ from starting His ministry, let alone finishing it! The scheme of Satan to devour Jesus clearly centered on invalidation, hoping to render the Lord weak in nature, inferior in devotion and useless in ministry.

Throughout church history some, including Martin Luther, spoke of the enemy's schemes as misbeliefs. How accurate, for lies compose untrue thoughts containing values or beliefs which form ungodly character and generate evil behavior. As seen, misbeliefs originate from the devil who in scripture is known as the father of lies: Jesus declared to those who rejected him, "*You belong to your father, the devil, and you want to carry out your father's desire. He was a murderer from the beginning, not holding to the truth, for there is no truth in him. When he lies, he speaks his native language, for he is a liar and the father of lies.*" (John 8:44) Everything untrue or deceptive is a lie, a misbelief which ultimately comes from Satan. We may learn and adopt misbeliefs as part of our value system, stemming from the influence of family, friends, teachers, coaches, bosses, books, websites, advertisements, magazines ... anybody, anything and anywhere. Satan is a liar!

The devil's lies have impacted the best of people. For instance, I sat amazed in the restaurant as my closest confidant blurted out, "I don't feel validated by you!" Questions raced through my head as I wondered what he was talking about. I knew he blamed me for something, but for what? As time passed clarity broke through. Suffering low self-esteem, he grasped love from me that I could not possibly provide. He longed to experience a sense of worth from someone and the only someone who could give that was the Great Someone, God.

How often friends, spouses, and co-workers might look to us (and us to them) to meet a heart-felt need only God can fulfill. This proved to be the case when my friend e-mailed me and others a few years later, explaining his quest for validation ... a deprivation of caring throughout childhood. Getting in touch with the cause of his inner pain, he now asked forgiveness from the group of e-mail recipients, knowing he placed an unrealistic expectation upon us. Putting God's face on people is a scheme of Satan cleverly implemented to produce relational disappointment. I am glad my friend identified the misbelief in his thought patterns (needing validation from me), uncovered the root of false thinking (rejection during pre-adolescence), and humbly pursued reconciliation (his e-mail desiring forgiveness).

Some years previous I went through a similar struggle, a challenging but eye-opening time I'll never forget. Fortunately I received spiritual guidance from Bill, my mentor in the late 1970's, with whom I met every Wednesday for greasy barbeque and godly counsel. Bill owned and managed a commercial construction company which required great business savvy. Moreover, he was a man of spiritual wisdom. Knowing I had been frustrated with my boss, one day Bill told me, "Whatever you receive from people is just icing on the cake." In other words, Jesus is the Whole Cake! He is the only source who can satisfy the innermost needs and yearnings of our hearts. Our spouse can't, our boyfriend or girlfriend can't, our friends can't, our boss can't, our pastor can't and our church can't. Why? Because people are human and incomplete. But Jesus is divine and perfect. He even knows our needs before we ask.

What's my point? Don't give people power over your life! Don't let others determine how you feel, what you perceive about yourself, or how you will respond. Don't fall into the trap of invalidation! Even if people affirm you or encourage you, their kind words merely represent the icing. Thank them. But remember your sense of worth has already been decided. Jesus came to earth for you, died for you, conquered death for you, and now prepares heaven for you. You are validated as a child of God! You are worth dying for. No one can change that, not even Satan with his scheme of lies.

So how do we respond when Satan tempts us with this scheme? Just as Jesus did. We resist the devil. After the warning to be self-controlled and alert because the devil prowls around looking for someone to devour, Peter wrote, *"Resist him!"* (1 Peter 5:9) Resistance involves recognizing the lie as a lie. Thoughts of invalidation include the following lies: I am unlovable. I am stupid. I am worthless. I am a failure. I am ugly. I have nothing to offer. I should quit. These demoralizing misbeliefs must be called what they are, lies from the father of lies.

Resistance also requires replacing the lie with the truth. Truthful thoughts, in alignment with scripture, include: I am unconditionally loved by Jesus (Romans 5:8). I am made in the image of God (Genesis 2:27). I am a temple of the Holy Spirit (1 Corinthians 6:19). I have abilities from the Lord to serve Him and His church (1 Peter 4:10). Resisting temptation is not complicated. Just be vulnerable, willing to admit when you are tempted and/or when you've bought into a lie. Identify it and then cast it off as you replace falsehood with truth. Only truth will set you free from the schemes of Satan.

Obviously, the importance of reading the Bible cannot be over-emphasized. If we don't journey on a regular basis through the inspired Word of God, we will de-sensitize ourselves from the lies of Satan which run rampant in our society and sometimes in our own head. Unalert, we will lose self-control. Conversely, if we fill our minds with spiritual truth we will remain sensitive to misbeliefs, able to lay them aside as schemes of our enemy. The inerrant wisdom of scripture will keep us safe. Safe from expecting validation from others. Safe from accepting invalidation from Satan. Validation, our sense of worth, only comes from heaven. God loves you. In Jesus He validated you, demonstrating His love, your worth. No more searching.

Chapter 1
Discussion Questions

1. Why is scripture our defense to overcome temptation?

2. How would you rank yourself (on a scale of 1-10) pertaining to the 1 Peter 5:8 qualities of self-control and alertness? (1 weakest, 10 strongest)

3. How has Satan tried to invalidate you as a child, teenager, adult? How did you respond? What were the results?

4. Did you ever put God's face on someone, looking to them instead of God for validation of your personal worth? What happened?

5. What scriptures have kept you, or could keep you, from giving in to the scheme of invalidation?

Chapter 2

Isolation

"The Bible knows nothing of solitary religion."
John Wesley

*I*f Satan fails with the scheme of invalidation do not be surprised by his common ploy of isolation. In other words, if our enemy can't discredit us through misbeliefs about ourselves, watch out for his objective to pull us away from Christians who consistently remind us of our value to God. Did you know Americans are more isolated and, therefore, more lonely than ever before? According to the American Sociological Review, in 1985 the average American maintained three relationships in which they shared matters important to them. However, by 2004 (less than 20 years later) 80% of Americans confided in no one, with the possible exception of a close family member.[1]

How could this drastic change occur in such a short period? Recall 1 Peter 5:8. Satan prowls around like a roaring lion looking for someone to devour. And how does a lion execute strategy to conquer its subject? Isolation! After spotting a pack of animals a lion will quietly stalk them, determining which one seems most vulnerable, usually one who is ill and/or walking at the back of the herd. Then the lion waits until that animal separates from its protective group or can be drawn away. Once isolated, the subject has little or no chance of survival as the lead attacker with its accompanying family (called a pride) asphyxiates or at least feasts on the prey until it dies.

Isolation is the scheme. The subject loses all protection when it wanders off. Although a lion or lioness will assail a variety of herds, they generally ignore giraffes since giraffes travel in clusters called kinships, groups committed to watching out for one another ... safety in numbers!

So it is with us. Satan watches for the opportune moment when we are weak spiritually, emotionally, or physically. Then he lures us away from fellowship, particularly our church and group of Christian friends who know us the best and love us the most. Now he has us where he wants us, alone and vulnerable, isolated! No surprise, therefore, that scripture exhorts Christians, *"Let us not give up meeting together, as some are in the habit of doing, but let us encourage one another..."* (Hebrews 10:25)

The biblical pattern for meeting together, inspired by the Holy Spirit poured out at Pentecost to birth the church, was two-fold. The early disciples gathered publicly in the temple area as a congregation and privately in their homes as small groups.

"Day after day, in the temple courts and from house to house, they never stopped teaching and proclaiming the good news that Jesus is the Christ." (Acts 5: 42) Both contexts served as teaching and preaching outposts, and there was more: *"[42]They devoted themselves to the apostles' teaching and to the fellowship, to the breaking of bread and to prayer. [43]Everyone was filled with awe, and many wonders and miraculous signs were done by the apostles. [44]All the believers were together and had everything in common. [45]Selling their possessions and goods, they gave to anyone as he had need. [46]Every day they continued to meet together in the temple courts. They broke bread in their homes and ate together with glad and sincere hearts, [47]praising God and enjoying the favor of all the people. And the Lord added to their number daily those who were being saved."* (Acts 2:42-47)

The early church established a profoundly unique presence as their relationships displayed the love Jesus taught and modeled, mutual caring of a depth never seen before. Together the disciples remembered the death of Christ in celebrating the Lord's Supper, petitioned God for answers in prayer, experienced power to do miracles, shared meals and communion in the intimacy of their homes, praised God for all His blessings, enjoyed the favor of those around them, and welcomed new Christians into the church on a daily basis.

How could all this happen? The church devoted themselves to one another (verse 42). Devoted to fellowship as a natural result of loving Jesus, these Christ-followers served as a conduit to meet each others' needs. They cared for one another as the Lord cared for them, even selling possessions for money to share with those in need. In this Spirit-initiated environment a wall of protection surrounded the family of believers. *"Love always protects."* (1 Corinthians 13:7) And here that love held the disciples in the center of God's will, safe from the scheme of isolation.

Devotion protects us, isolation endangers us. Devotion strengthens us, isolation weakens us. Whereas devotion to fellowship guards us from the influence of Satan, isolation from fellowship exposes us to the influence of Satan. Therefore, we must make every effort to keep meeting together so we will *"spur one another on toward love and good deeds."* (Hebrews 10:24) We must not neglect the godly habit of congregational and small group fellowship so we can consistently encourage one another. It's biblical. It's Holy Spirit ordained. It's for our good.

Like the animal which separates from the pack and jeopardizes its safety, some Christians commit the same mistake. For a variety of reasons we might neglect the habit of fellowship. We feel tired, we take on too much work, we let our children participate in too many activities, we prioritize a television show or athletic game, we don't want others to know our weaknesses, we keep hiding our secret sin, we stop studying the Bible, we think we have no spiritual gifts to offer, we don't like being around a particular person, we fail to pray regularly, we pressure ourselves to finish home projects, we give in to our introverted personality, we discount our spiritual growth, we dislike the time of the gathering or the weather that day. The result? We make ourselves unduly vulnerable. Cutting ourselves out of the safety net of Christian community, where we experience the love of Jesus, the encouragement of the Holy Spirit and the grace of God, compromises our spiritual devotion and risks our spiritual health.

Elaine, a sweet young lady loved by everyone, enjoyed giving time and energy to help others, anytime and anywhere. Her merciful heart gravitated toward the needy, ready to pray for them and cry with them. Anyone would feel comforted and encouraged by her in a period of difficulty or turmoil. She cared and showed it. Over the course of time, however, Elaine lost touch with her self, her personal needs and significant relationships. She paid little attention to her marriage, parenting, friendships, and church. The longer and wider she responded to cries for help, the deeper the gap grew between her and the most important people in her life. Not aware of why she felt so empty, after all she loved God passionately and served Him constantly, weakness set in. Sadness took root.

Soon her times alone with God, praying and studying scripture, decreased in frequency. Communication at home turned argumentative and combative. Parenting changed from a blessing to an obligation. Elaine didn't want to burden others with her flattened emotional state and struggles at home. She withdrew. And life spiraled out of control.

Separating from the stability of her long-term rela-tionships in the church, Elaine cast aside people who could pray with her and cry with her. She shut down. Within months nothing was going in and nothing was going out. Her soul became stagnant. She stood alone, walked alone, and felt alone.

Then it happened. A flirtatious man at her work-place turned his attention toward Elaine. Void of close relationship at home and now in the church as well, would she resist the thoughts of adultery? No. In her weakness Satan stalked her, lured her away from caring relationships and devoured her. Elaine lost her wonderful husband, their 3 children, their new home, her job, her church, her extended family, her ministry, her friends, her sweet spirit and her closeness with God. How? Isolation! The devil capitalized on her weakness. No fellowship, no protection.

Referring to our spiritual enemy, Jesus proclaimed, *"The thief comes only to steal and kill and destroy."* (John 10:10) The best of people get blindsided when they distance themselves from those who know them best and love them most. Isolation is one of the most common tricks in the devil's bag. Don't go there! Remain in the safety of a caring community of fellow Christians. Open your life and pour out your heart, especially in a time of weakness. In John 10:10 Jesus also said, *"I have come that they may have life, and have it to the full."* Fellowship, which includes letting others in on our major concerns, decisions, temptations, and weaknesses, will protect the life we have in Christ so we can have life as He purposed, life to the full. Go there. Enjoy an extraordinary life. Devote yourself to fellowship!

The most transformational moments of my life occurred in small group settings. As a young man seeking guidance for my future, the Lord used my small group to help direct me toward a ministry of teaching scripture. Subsequently I received under-graduate and graduate training. And now I've taught the Bible for the past 35 years. Looking back, I'm sure thankful for the prayer and encouragement of my small group, mutually devoted to fellowship. There I discovered the overall purpose for my life.

Another pivotal time came when I was sick with an undiagnosed illness. In addition to my small group praying, I asked 6 people to pray together for me, an hour each week at my office. Their caring prayers and spiritual insight sustained me for many months until an accurate diagnosis and proper medication brought healing. I don't know how I would have persevered without their love for me.

I am out to change isolated Christians to devoted Christians, copying the New Testament pattern like John Wesley did in his era. Developing small groups called "bands," "classes" and "societies," he proclaimed his conviction to the masses: "The Bible knows nothing of solitary religion." On behalf of the church, he resisted the temptation to isola-tion. As this scheme of Satan was broken, genuine revival took place. My dream for all Christians, then, is consistent participation not only in large church gatherings, but also in small group meetings where mutual caring catalyzes one another into deeper relationship and renewal throughout the church.

Renewal is a together thing: *"Now you are the body of Christ, and each one of you is a part of it."* (1 Corinthians 12:27) The "body of Christ" metaphor describes the church. It is a living organism of which individual Christians comprise a vital part, together representing Jesus to the world ... like the fullness of the physical body with its many individual parts connecting in health, unity and purpose. As in the physical, every member of the spiritual body, the church, remains crucial. Therefore, the body is not something you attend, it's something you are! You have a part to play. In fact, you are indispensable. The church can't afford isolated Christians.

Solomon, the wisest man in his time, helps explain your significance in the church. *"Iron sharpens iron, so one man sharpens another."* (Proverbs 27:17) During this period of history, a sword was created by pounding a piece of iron with an iron hammer, flattening it around the edges like thin sheet metal. Then an iron file was utilized to make a razor-like edge, deadly in battle.[2] As iron sharpens iron, so Christians sharpen Christians. We hone each other into the shape and purpose of God for shared spiritual victories against the schemes of Satan.

This takes place through various means. Recall Hebrews 10:24-25: *"Let us consider how we may spur one another on to love and good deeds. Let us not give up meeting together, as some are in the habit of doing, but let us encourage one another..."* The simple words and actions of encouragement spur fellow-Christians forward to love like Jesus loves and serve like Jesus serves. But we need that encouragement. We need the church. We need one another. We cannot be both the thin piece of iron and the hammer. We cannot be both the thin piece of iron and the file. We must have devoted fellowship, uniting with other Christ-followers to sharpen one another with acute sensitivity, ready and able to cut through the lies of our enemy including his scheme of isolation.

Don't neglect fellowship, then. Don't stay home. Meet together and encourage one another, following the model of the New Testament church. Congregate with your local church and come together in a small group. It's not only the two-fold biblical pattern of fellowship in the Acts church; it's the will of God initiated by the power of the Holy Spirit for the glory of Jesus. The Acts church is the model church. It's the church God planned. In this church the scheme of isolation has no power over you.

Chapter 2
Discussion Questions

1. In your opinion, what change would help transform the American church into an Acts church?

2. Describe the blessings you've experienced through fellowship in a small group?

3. What could your small group do in order to look more like the devoted fellowship observed in Acts 2:42-47?

4. How could you improve in spurring others on in love and good deeds?

5. Have you been tempted by the scheme of isolation? If so, what circumstances surrounded that time? How did you handle the temptation to pull away from other Christians?

Chapter 3

Indulgence

"Desire only God, and your heart will be satisfied."
Augustine

During an interview in 2009 Tiger Woods said, "Being a father is the most significant thing I've ever done. People say I was born to play golf, but I think I was born to be a dad."[1] The best golfer in the world, and maybe in the history of the sport, appeared to have a healthy perspective on balancing life at work and life at home. More importantly, he seemed to care deeply about his family. But then the shocking news hit the internet, television, radio, and every newspaper in America. Tiger not only wrecked his vehicle in his own driveway, but the internationally esteemed sports hero also wrecked his family.

Accused of multiple adulterous relationships, this shining star who had a beautiful wife, 2 wonderful children, a mansion in Florida, hundreds of millions in endorsement dollars, and a net worth in the billions, started to fade behind a dark closet full of allegations. This story was so scandalous—a man with everything imaginable that an earthly life could offer, yet carrying on a secret life of indulgence—it covered the front page of some national newspapers longer than the 9/11 terrorist attacks! Crowned the "athlete of the decade" for 2000 to 2010, even indulgent society couldn't help but crown him "cheater of the decade."

To his credit, Tiger Woods eventually owned responsibility for betraying his spouse and family. Nevertheless, he lost his wife through divorce and consequently lost full access to his children. This sad story begs the question, "How did this happen?" Did he wake up one day with a sexual addiction? Of course not. Rather, he woke up one day and had a thought about cheating on his wife, a thought with the potential to devour. And it did. Tiger gave in to indulgence, a blatant and prevalent scheme of Satan.

Indulgence raises its voice emphatically, "I can have what I want," "I deserve what I want." This attitude of entitlement permeates American culture now more than ever, elevating self-centeredness above all. The Bible predicted this 2,000 years ago: *"But mark this: There will be terrible times in the last days. People will be lovers of themselves, lovers of money, boastful, proud, abusive, disobedient to their parents, ungrateful, unholy, without love, unforgiving, slanderous, without self-control, brutal, not lovers of the good, treacherous, rash, conceited, lovers of pleasure rather than lovers of God—having a form of godliness but denying its power. Have nothing to do with them."* (2 Timothy 3:1-5)

The last days appear to be upon us, for love of pleasure dominates the world in stark contrast to love of God. Self-indulgent sins like greed, deception and pornography run rampant. Sadly, even some who call themselves Christian look little or nothing like Christ. Certainly Jesus never invited us to an attitude of entitlement which fosters sins of indulgence. Rather, He issued a challenge: *"If anyone wants to be first, he must be the very last and the servant of all."* (Mark 9:35) Self-indulgence cuts across the grain of everything Christian. Realize, then, we can't even begin to follow Jesus until we die to a lifestyle of self-centeredness, losing our way of life for His.

A self-centered life for some looks like entertainment overload. We indulge self by roaming the internet without cause, incessantly looking through Facebook, watching innumerable movies, staring at television shows for hours on end, playing games on our phones when we have a minute to spare, texting unmeaningful messages throughout the day, or mastering video games. Inordinate time and effort wasted forever. I'm not anti-entertainment. However, entertainment morphs into a false god when it captures our attention to the expense of knowing Jesus, loving Jesus, and following Jesus. Many might believe Christ died on a cross, but what does that mean? That we are set free to entertain ourselves?

Surely some find a balance when it comes to entertainment, but others watch television 4 or 5, even 8 hours a day. And what about Facebook?

The norm for 90 million American users is 4 hours and 39 minutes daily.[2] This is not balance, let alone Christ-like. This can be called nothing but purpose-less, frivolous indulgence. You may not fit this statistical mold, but let me ask if you are over-dosing on entertainment to the detriment of loving Jesus with all your heart, soul, strength and mind? Are you focusing on activities that prevent you from loving others like Jesus loves you? These questions represent the two greatest commandments according to Christ (Matthew 22:37-39 and John 13:34). Along with all temptations, the scheme of indulgence tries to draw us away from adherence to these primary commands.

Pornography unquestionably diverts our attention from the biblical commands to love. The devil whispers, "Put your eyes on this ... Take a look at her ... Click on that picture ... Check it out." Is it any wonder the pornographic industry rakes in 14 billion dollars annually in the U.S. alone, capitalizing on 4.2 million pornographic web sites, drawing 40 million visitors daily.[3] Satan strategizes to fix our attention on objects of lust thereby capturing hearts and leaving no time, energy, or desire to love God and love others. Indulgence crafted by our enemy who steals, kills, and destroys.

In large part, the devil has already stolen the morality of our nation. Our politicians set the tone of indulgence with adultery, tax-evasion, sexual deviations, unethical expenditures, and on and on ad nauseam. Former Senator John Edwards fathered a child with his mistress during his wife's battle against cancer. While Edwards ran for presidential candidate, his associate tried to take the fall, claiming he was the real father of the baby. Now investigation ensues concerning an unimaginable amount of illegal funds allegedly utilized by Edwards to cover up his sexual affair and the birth of his child.

While John Edwards leads the recent parade of indulgence in governmental circles, Arnold Schwarzenegger follows close behind with his sexual escapades. Also, Eliot Spitzer resigns as New York Governor for involvement as client number 9 in a prostitution ring. And most recently, Anthony Weiner steps down from Congress after admitting he sent explicit sexual messages and photos to a number of women over a 3 year period. A sad display of deception and perversion.

Where will all the indulgence stop? Sadly, not in the church ... at least yet. Christianity Today reports there is little difference between Christian teens' sexual behavior and that of non-Christian youth.[4] Should this surprise us when 50% of Christian men and 20% of Christian women admit to being addicted to pornography?[5] Where are the spiritual examples for our children?

Pornography essentially turns people into products, no longer respected, only consumed. It redefines men and women, created in the image of God, as commodities—usable, dispensable, unlovable. Holding people hostage in virtual reality does not occur without devastating consequences to the human spirit. Porn offers sex-slaves to the viewer and in his heart the viewer stands convicted of human-trafficking. Adults must step up to objective moral standards for the morality of America could be forever forsaken.

Regrettably, many adults leading our institutions of higher learning facilitate this path of destruction. Sex Week at Yale has popularized similar events at universities across the country with sessions including porn stars, stripping lessons, orgasm seminars, and sex toy demonstrations. The University of Missouri-Kansas City's sex fair was fully endorsed by Associate Vice Chancellor for Student Affairs: "The sex program was approved based on the educational value the event brings to the participants."[6] A few years ago another college, formerly a Christian school, adopted a resolution in favor of open distribution of condoms on campus. Why the change? Campus leaders held several talks with students and reviewed a student report on sexual health. Is this education?

C.S. Lewis, a truly educated man, wrote, "Education without values ... seems rather to make man a more clever devil."[7] Satan infatuates and seduces the educated whose research abandons virtue and whose enlightenment blinds common sense. Education apart from spiritual values results in arrogance and indulgence ... a more clever devil.

The habit of indulgence is not just bad. It's a sinful pattern that forfeits heaven: *"Do you not know that the wicked will not inherit the kingdom of God? Do not be deceived: Neither the sexually Immoral nor idolaters nor adulterers nor male prostitutes nor homosexual offenders nor thieves nor the greedy nor drunkards nor slanderers nor swindlers will inherit the kingdom of God."* (1 Corinthians 6:9-10) The kingdom of God depicts the reign of Jesus, the King of God's kingdom, in the hearts of men and women. Therefore, Jesus rules over the heart of a Christian. The enemy, the devil, rules over the heart of an indulger. We choose who rules.

If we decide to turn the control of our life over to Christ, we experience God's kingdom now, on earth. We then live for the will of our King and confidently expect the fullness of God's kingdom in heaven. The dividing line is not complicated. Have we repented of our sins and invited Jesus to establish the kingdom of God in us? Are we currently seeking, knowing, and following His kingly direction? Are we growing in our love for Him and for others?

An attitude of entitlement, of course, refuses to bow before the King. We want what we want. And we get just that, life void of His reign. So we go on looking to be served through the indulgence of entertainment, sex, materialism, whatever. The lie permeating this attitude says, "I deserve good, I deserve better, I deserve more." The lie must be replaced with the truth that we are here not to be served, but to serve. Life is not about us. Life is Jesus.

Jesus makes it simple. We will experience victory over the scheme of indulgence only when we consistently serve others: *"If someone forces you to go one mile, go with him two miles."* (Matthew 5:41) Let me explain. During the Roman Empire a soldier in the Roman legion could legally require anyone to carry his armor one mile. When walking long distances across the country, then, a soldier would often place this demand on a person from each town through which his legion traveled. This gave the Roman soldier a break from bearing the weight of his shield (about 20 lbs.), his protective clothing (about 30 lbs.) and other pieces including a helmet. At the end of this mile the soldier would resume wearing or transporting his armor. Or, he could try to enlist another person to do so.

What Jesus meant, then, in saying, "Go with him two miles," is this: Surprise people with a willing heart to serve, going beyond what is required. Be like a Roman citizen, who after fulfilling his duty would unexpectedly say, "I'll carry your armor an additional mile!" How astonishing, how unusual. Jesus not only denounced entitlement here in Matthew 5:41, He also implored Christians to give of themselves above and beyond the normal standard of service. So, be unusual. Be an exception to the rule. Forget yourself and serve and then serve some more. *"Your attitude should be the same as that of Christ Jesus: Who, being in very nature God, did not consider equality with God something to be grasped, but made himself nothing, taking the very nature of a servant, being made in human likeness."* (Philippians 2:5-7)

Two years ago a little girl in our church was diagnosed with a brain tumor. Many of us prayed for her and supported the family in a variety of ways. Let me tell you what two sisters did (age 8 and 11) when they gained some understanding of the medical costs involved. They held a game day in the basement of their home. They created flyers and distributed them, letting people know that the admission fee to game day would fully go toward the little girl's medical expenses. Eighty people showed up and in just a few hours they collected $1,000. If an 8 year old and an 11 year old can serve like this, certainly we can go the extra mile as well.

How many people do you know who feel entitled to a better job, or better pay, or better cars, or better marriage, or better home, or better vacation, or better sex? Are you one of them? If so, let go of that attitude. It's a scheme of Satan who wants to distract you, detour you, discourage you, and then devour you. Turn off the lies of entitlement: "I have the right to ..." "I deserve ..." "Everybody else has ..." Replace lies with the truth: "God knows what I need." "I can trust Him." "God has in mind my best interests." "I am free to serve, not to be served." Leave indulgence, life centered on you. Embrace service, life centered on Jesus. Let the King of God's kingdom rule in your heart. Then you will be free, free indeed from the scheme of indulgence.

Chapter 3
Discussion Questions

1. In one sentence summarize Satan's scheme of indulgence.

2. Besides entertainment overload and sexual immorality, what are some other avenues of self-indulgence?

3. Share an example of someone whose education, apart from values, made them more susceptible to the devil's lies. (No names please.)

4. Why do habitual sins of indulgence preclude one from heaven?

5. Tell about a time when you felt entitled to something. What was it? How did you respond? What were the results?

6. How does serving others minimize sins of indulgence?

Chapter 4

Idealism

"There is nothing we can do to make God love us more. There is nothing we can do to make God love us less." Philip Yancey

*I*f Satan can't make us feel bad about ourselves (invalidation), pull us away from fellowship (isolation), or draw us into selfishness (indulgence), he may try his scheme of idealism. Idealism is the misbelief that we must be perfect in order to gain acceptance. A cruel taskmaster, perfectionism pushes us toward unrealistic standards in a merciless fashion. Those who have succumbed to idealism likely had a perfectionistic role model.

I had at least two, my parents. Although well-meaning, their expectations were beyond my reach. I couldn't stay clean enough. I couldn't keep my room neat enough. I couldn't dress nice enough. And I couldn't cut my hair short enough! My father's standards were primarily implanted in me through athletics. He starred in basketball and baseball, then signed a contract to play professional baseball after graduating from high school. Despite lots of success in the same sports, my efforts seemed to go unnoticed. Without appropriate reinforcement, whether positive words or physical affection, liability to the scheme of idealism increased. I tried harder and worked longer to achieve his acceptance. But I struggled in vain.

When I became a Christian at age 19, I knew Jesus loved me and accepted me unconditionally, but my upbringing and subsequent perceptions blocked the experience of God's grace in my daily life. For years I subconsciously bought into the lies of Satan prodding me to be better and do better, to perform, to earn love's acceptance which can't be earned. Imperative thoughts plagued me: "You must never make a mistake." "You have to do this work now." "You can't stop until you're done." "You should be perfect."

Then one day I read Psalm 37:3, *"Trust in the Lord and do good,"* and saw it in a whole new light. Previously I lived and worked with the compulsive drive to do good. And whatever I couldn't take care of or finish, well, I'd have to trust the Lord for those circumstances or responsibilities. But God revealed that I had it backwards. I read it as "Do good and trust in the Lord," putting me in charge instead of God. No wonder I felt stressed out each day. I had submitted to the Christian cliché, "Do your best and trust God with the rest." That's just wrong.

The turnaround proved more than freeing.

My joy level shot up as I daily acknowledged God as sovereign and acquiesced control, leaving the burden of perfectionism at His feet. He is perfect, I am not. He is God, I am not. Now I trust the Lord, doing what I believe He desires instead of doing what I believe I should. Because I am not perfect I don't trust Him perfectly. But His grace is enough. His acceptance is unconditional. Therefore, He does not get down on me. Plus, He does not give me more than I can do, does not push me to complete the things He desires, does not expect perfection in doing His will, and does not stress me out along the path of trusting Him. This is the acceptance we all need.

Idealism constructs an unending road of futility for no one leads a flawless life. That's why we need to place our trust in the perfection of Jesus. If a Christian, we did so at the point of repentance, confessing our sinfulness to God, embracing forgiveness from Christ, and receiving power through the Holy Spirit … transformed from a performance-oriented person to a grace-oriented person. And once we experience unconditional acceptance through His amazing grace, we keep on living like this: *"Just as you received Christ Jesus as Lord, continue to live in Him."* (Colossians 2:6)

In other words, we continue to trust in the Lord just as we did on the day of our salvation. On that day of becoming a Christian we recognized we could do nothing apart from Jesus. We were lost. We repented. Everyday as a Christ-follower is the same. We rely on His grace-filled acceptance, putting our trust in Him, knowing without Him we are nothing and can do nothing of eternal value. So idealism is a lie. We didn't earn acceptance and never will. Therefore, live like you did when you were born again. Walk like you walked when you stepped into God's kingdom. Accept your acceptance!

The apostle Peter was tripped up by the scheme of idealism from time to time, once when he accompanied Jesus to a mountaintop. *"After six days Jesus took with him Peter, James and John the brother of James, and led them up a high mountain by themselves. There he was transfigured before them. His face shone like the sun, and his clothes became as white as the light. Just then there appeared before them Moses and Elijah, talking with Jesus. Peter said to Jesus, 'Lord, it is good for us to be here. If you wish, I will put up three shelters—one for you, one for Moses and one for Elijah.' While he was still speaking, a bright cloud enveloped them, and a voice from the cloud said, 'This is my Son, whom I love; with him I am well pleased. Listen to him!'"* (Matthew 17:1-5)

When Jesus transformed from human appearance to heavenly appearance, Peter immediately came up with a plan that seemed ideal, constructing three buildings to house Moses, Elijah, and Jesus. Surely this would honor each one and possibly create a sacred place. Think of it! People could come from all over Judea to have a mountaintop encounter with these three. According to Mark's account, however, Peter was reacting to the miracle rather than responding to Christ. Therefore, God's voice interrupts Peter's idealistic proposal: *"This is my*

Son, whom I love; with Him I am well pleased. Listen to Him." At this, Peter (and James and John) fell face-down in fear. This is the response that should have occurred when the appearance of Jesus changed. Peter should have fallen prostrate before the Lord in worship, but he wanted to honor Jesus with a house. God wanted Peter to honor Jesus with his heart.

Idealism initiates ideas that appear ideal. God's ideas, though, are grounded in reality, a reality that is heavenly orchestrated, not humanly conceived. Exactly like the transfiguration of Jesus, a God-thing, not something man designed. Just imagine if Peter's wish would have been granted, at best causing a delay to the crucifixion. Idealism is not really ideal.

On another occasion Jesus warned of Satan's strategy to thwart Peter's dedication. Peter swiftly answered, *"Lord, I am ready to go with you to prison and to death."* (Luke 22:33) An admirable defense, idealism yes, but without considering the cost of identification with the Savior about to be arrested and crucified. The result? Three times Peter denied ever knowing Jesus.

To recognize the scheme of idealism we need to examine our motivation, execution, and attitude. Motivation refers to what mobilizes us internally, obligation or freedom, suspicion or trust, pleasing people or pleasing God. Regarding motivation we ask, "Am I led by the Holy Spirit or the Holy Should?" The Holy Spirit leads us peacefully and joyfully. Conversely, the Holy Should drives us anxiously and stressfully. Why? Because "we should" do such and such. We "have to!" The imperative nature of the

Holy Should doesn't let up, gives no slack, has no grace. Like riding a horse with no reins, we are out of control in search for acceptance. We are driven by obligation with the hope of looking good. On the other hand, the Holy Spirit leads us in freedom and trust, releasing us to glorify Jesus. No need here to search for acceptance. That was settled at the cross.

Execution involves the external practicalities of putting into action what motivates us. A life-changing principle I learned from Christian leaders about execution commends the scheduling of priorities instead of prioritizing a schedule. Idealism leans toward organizing, getting all our ducks in a row, to the expense of prioritizing the most significant responsibilities. In this mode we become slaves to our schedules. Schedules are good, but putting the truly important on our schedules requires weekly, daily and momentary reflection, asking directional questions such as: "What are the Lord's objectives for my day?" "What am I doing, or planning to do, that someone else could do?" "Am I doing God's will or merely marking things off my list?" "What is the big picture here?" "Who would be best at responding to this need?" "How can I most productively extend the kingdom of God?" Raising the right questions will raise your schedule to a higher road of honoring Jesus. You won't just finish assignments, projects, lists or goals. You will live and move and have your being in the will of God (Acts 17:28).

Whereas motivation concerns itself with mobilizing factors and execution with prioritizing decisions, attitude forms the mindset we exhibit toward others while carrying out responsibilities. Since idealism revolves around doing our duty and pleasing others, we feel overwhelmed by a constant stream of "have to's". As a result, we wear out physically and emotionally, throwing us into a state of spiritual disequilibrium. Our attitude turns from caring to critical. And our imperative lifestyle, led by the Holy Should, creates a "life is hard" perspective.

Surely life presents difficulties, but the scheme of idealism traps us in a negative mind-set wherein we become hard on ourselves. And to the degree we are hard on ourselves, to that degree we are hard on others. We can only give away what we have and what we have is a critical outlook. Relationships suffer. We project our unrealistic expectations onto others which they can't meet. Blaming begins and we may end up bitter toward those who "let us down."

Grace frames a different picture. We move forward motivated by the Spirit. Responsibilities are executed by trusting in God. And Jesus stands glorified in our attitude. We may not be ideal for no one reaches perfection, but we rest in our acceptance by God and graciously give away the love with which He has loved us in the perfect sacrifice of Jesus on the cross.

I'll never forget a story which demonstrated grace so vividly. Thomas Jefferson and his companions, while traveling on horseback, approached a swollen river which had flooded its banks and washed away the bridge.[1] Each rider forded the rising waters on their horse, risking life as they fought against the rapid currents.

A traveler, who was not part of Jefferson's group, stepped aside to watch. After the first few made it safely to the other side, the stranger asked the President to ferry him across the waters. Jefferson agreed without hesitation. So the man joined the President on his horse and soon they arrived, without harm, on the far side of the flooded river.

Then one of Jefferson's companions inquired why the stranger asked the President for this meaningful favor. The man was shocked, admitting he had no idea his request was directed to the President of the United States. "All I know," he said, "is that on some of your faces was written the answer 'no' and on some of your faces was the answer 'yes.' His was a 'yes' face."

Sometimes people approach me, anxiously longing for a flawless life as a Christian. They ask, "What if I fall?" "What happens if I make a mistake?" These questions rise out of idealism. These folks don't need unrealistic assurance that they can lead a perfect or next-to-perfect life. What they really need is genuine acceptance, a gut-level understanding that no matter what occurs the Lord loves them completely and unconditionally. No hesitation. God has a "yes" face. His grace is enough.

The scheme of idealism engineers a trap in which many find themselves today. At times it feels unbearable. I know. The fight for earthly acceptance robs us of joy and saps our energy, restraining the Lordship of Christ in the here and now. Emotional turbulence precludes quietness of heart and calmness of soul.

Relational strife supersedes the commandment to *"love each other as I have loved you."* (John 15:22) A critical spirit blocks out the authentic caring of our Savior and God, Jesus Christ, and we can end up unhappy with ourselves and others. Avoid Satan's scheme by surrendering the pride of perfection- ism. When Jesus said, *"Be perfect, therefore, as your heavenly Father is perfect"* (Matthew 5:48), He did not demand a life without mistakes. The word "perfect" means mature, so continue to grow in grace and let go of unrealistic standards. Idealism is not ideal, it's a clever trick of the devil.

Chapter 4
Discussion Questions

1. Did you have a perfectionistic role model at home, in school, or elsewhere? If so, what was the primary misbelief they modeled for you?

2. How has that scheme of idealism influenced you?

3. When are you most vulnerable to being led by the Holy Should instead of the Holy Spirit?

4. How has God's grace enabled you to accept yourself, even when falling short of expectations?

5. How can you help others escape the lies of idealism?

Chapter 5

Ignorance

"Knowledge is the treasure of a wise man."
William Penn

"*I*t is better not to know so much than to know so many things that just ain't so."[1] Taking this folksy statement to heart, a college professor set out to evaluate his students. How much did they know that just ain't so? His 86 question test elicited some surprising answers: Charles Darwin invented gravity. Ralph Nader is a baseball player. Christ lived in the sixteenth century. Sid Caesar was an early Roman emperor. Mark Twain invented the cotton gin. Dwight Eisenhower served as president in the seventeenth century. Socrates was an Indian chief. Camp David is in Israel.[2]

The alarming lack of knowledge about our world and its history parallels the ignorance of ultimate truth, the Bible. For example, 72% of Americans believe we are blessed so we can enjoy life as much as possible. 42% claim that, according to scripture, Jesus sinned.[3] The views of self-described Christians are even more disturbing. For instance, 58% doubt or strongly doubt that the Holy Spirit is a living entity.[4] In other words, nearly 6 out of 10 believers do not believe God's Spirit represents anything more than a symbol of His presence. In this vein, the Spirit of the living God is not living. He is not personal. He only portrays a distant God.

First century Christians, to whom the letter of Hebrews was written, also lacked spiritual knowledge: *"We have much to say about this, but it is hard to explain because you are slow to learn. In fact, though by this time you ought to be teachers, you need someone to teach you the elementary truths of God's word all over again. You need milk, not solid food! Anyone who lives on milk, being still an infant, is not acquainted with the teaching about righteousness. But solid food is for the mature, who by constant use have trained themselves to distinguish good from evil."* (Hebrews 5:11-14)

Although these Jews maintained allegiance to Jesus for a period of time, they were undisciplined and slow to learn. They should have been teaching those younger in the faith, but needed instruction once again in the foundational truths of Christianity. Like babies, they couldn't handle anything of substance. They modeled spiritual infancy instead of spiritual maturity. Therefore, the author urges them to grow up: *"Leave the elementary teachings about Christ, and go on to maturity, not laying again the foundation of repentance from acts that lead to death, and of faith in God, instruction about baptisms, the laying on of hands, the resurrection of the dead, and eternal judgment."* (Hebrews 6:1-2)

The problem? Spiritual ignorance. The answer? Knowledge of spiritual truth. Not unlike this group of Hebrew Christians, the church today holds little understanding of these simplistic aspects of Christian doctrine and practice. Think about it. How many do you know in your church who can give a clear and concise definition of repentance, faith, baptisms, the laying on of hands, the resurrection of the dead and eternal judgment? Could they even describe their own experience of repentance, faith and baptism to an unbeliever in an intelligible manner? Furthermore, could they lead an unbeliever into life-transforming repentance, faith and baptism?

Apart from relatively new Christians, those in the church who cannot answer these questions have fallen behind spiritually. Their growth has atrophied, or plateaued at best. Why? Maybe a deprivation of biblical teaching, a lack of genuine fellowship, or an absence of spiritual mentoring. Or possibly the simple reason is personal neglect of God's Word. Here disconcerting statistics prevail. Although a national study revealed two-thirds of professing Christians read their Bible and almost all active Christians do so, a mere 18% claimed to read the Bible daily. Of those who read the Bible, four out of ten did so once a month at maximum.[5] A biblically illiterate America is just what the devil planned, for without immersion in the truth we subject ourselves to Satan's schemes.

So don't succumb to ignorance! Gain spiritual knowledge. Fill yourself with truth. The Bible as truth is described in numerous passages. Consider the apostle Paul's words: *"All scripture is God-breathed and is useful for teaching, rebuking, correcting and training in righteousness."* (2 Timothy 3:16) "God-breathed" means the very life of God inspiring the written words of scripture. So when we read the Bible we are not only reading about life, we are ingesting life, life as truth, life as the Lord of the universe intended.

The great evangelist, Billy Graham, underscored the significance of God's Word when interviewed in the midst of his amazing world-wide ministry. He was asked, "If you had your life to live over again, what would you do differently?" He responded, "One of my great regrets is that I have not studied enough. I wish I had studied more and preached less."[6] How enlightening! The most powerful evangelist of the twentieth century confessed his need, a need for more of God's life flowing into him and through him—more teaching, more correction, more training—an increase of life on the higher plane of divine truth.

Billy Graham knew the secret which distinguishes a routine life from a remarkable life. God will not reveal Himself beyond the point of your willingness to enter the adventure of knowing Him. At what level, then, is your willingness to know God? His Word? Truth? Apart from the knowledge of His God-breathed Word, you cannot live the life meant for you. Life apart from the Bible doesn't work right.

Don't misunderstand. Scripture is not truth because it works. It works because it is truth. Os Guinness adds, "It is not simply true for us; it is true even if nobody believes it and falsehood is false even if everybody believes it."[7] This brings us to a fork in the road, a reality test. If truth is truth regardless of who accepts it and falsehood is false even if everyone ascribes to it, then we must choose. Will we follow truth, what is right? Or lies, what is wrong? God's revelation of truth or Satan's scheme of ignorance?

Reality test serves as an accurate descriptor here, for truth constitutes reality. Jesus declared to the Jews who had believed Him, *"If you hold to my teaching, you are really my disciples. Then you will know the truth, and the truth will set you free."* (John 8:31-32) The New Testament Greek word translated "truth" literally means reality. Therefore, those who accept and obey the words of Jesus (and the rest of scripture) live in reality! Yes, the essential nature of what God breathed out, truth, is ours today. And this truth sets us free to live on the highest level possible ... life as God intended, in the center of His will. In other words, God-breathed truth creates a reality which exists above mere human knowledge, perspectives, attitudes, opinions and behaviors. Christians are commanded to live for God, far surpassing a mundane and superficial existence.

So why do only 18% of Christians read the Bible daily? It's simple. Most prefer the artificial life they create for themselves rather than the higher reality God creates for them. This stirs up questions:

Are the other 82% genuine Christ-followers? How can they live the life God purposed if they don't carve out time to read His God-breathed will? Is this why the modern church pales in comparison to the powerful church observed in the book of Acts? No wonder former Secretary of State, William Bennett, concluded, "We have become the kind of society that civilized countries used to send missionaries to."[8]

Satan would have us do anything but read God's truth. Why? The devil not only blinds the spiritual eyes of unbelievers (2 Corinthians 4:4), his scheme includes deceiving believers and/or church attenders as well. Surveys over the last decade reveal that roughly half of mainline Protestants (Lutherans, Methodists, Presbyterians, etc.) don't even believe Satan exists. Ironically, about the same number of these people believe in UFO's. The scheme of ignorance engulfs those we know, scores of co-workers, neighbors, friends, family and church members. It's Satan in his most superb design: Let people go to church and at the same time cause them to doubt the existence of a spiritual enemy.

As the devil's lies get misconstrued as reality, people buy into a life that lacks God-intentioned meaning. They settle for fiddling with broken seashells when they could be riding on the height of waves. Stooping to ignorance, void of purpose, reality passes by. Consider homosexuality. Despite the fact only 2-3% of our population identify themselves as homosexual, why does this subject get so much time and attention from the media? Spiritual darkness. They don't understand the high priority of Satan to spread the deception that homosexuals should not only receive acceptance, but affirmation as well. Almost all media are not concerned with what is right anyway. They are concerned with what is tolerant ... the scheme of ignorance.

The truth of scripture, however, trains us in righteousness, what is right in God's eyes: *"[18]The wrath of God is being revealed from heaven against all the godlessness and wickedness of men who suppress the truth by their wickedness, [19]since what may be known about God is plain to them, because God has made it plain to them. [20]For since the creation of the world God's invisible qualities—His eternal power and divine nature—have been clearly seen, being understood from what has been made, so that men are without excuse. [21]For although they knew God, they neither glorified Him as God nor gave thanks to Him, but their thinking became futile and their foolish hearts were darkened. ... [25]They exchanged the truth of God for a lie, and worshiped and served created things rather than the Creator—who is forever praised. Amen. [26]Because of this, God gave them over to shameful lusts. Even their women exchanged natural relations for unnatural ones. [27]In the same way the men also abandoned natural relations with women and were inflamed with lust for one another. Men committed indecent acts with other men, and received in themselves the due penalty for their perversion. ... [32]Although they know God's righteous decree that those who do such things deserve death, they not only continue to do these very things but also approve of those who practice them."* (Romans 1:18-21, 25-27, 32)

Notice the progression of Satan's scheme. They suppressed the truth (vs. 18). Their thinking became futile (vs. 21). The truth of God was exchanged for a lie (vs. 25). They reaped what they sowed, i.e., same-sex relations (vss. 26-27). They continued to disobey God's truth and approve of others who joined them (vs. 32). Step by step the devil robs people of the truth so he can bankrupt them spiritually. He leaves them with an artificial life, which is no life at all. No reality.

Thank God, though, we can avoid the scheme of ignorance and flourish in our spirituality through His divinely inspired Word. I began the daily practice of reading the Bible at age 19, when I repented of my sins and dedicated myself to follow Christ. Since my early Christian experience I've rarely missed a day of personal Bible study. With full confidence I can say this spiritual habit has been the most instrumental means of shaping my life as a disciple of Jesus. Let me offer, then, a few guidelines that helped me maximize spiritual growth and minimize spiritual ignorance throughout many years as a Christian. The following can also be found in my book, "Authentic Christianity—Starting Strong and Staying Strong."

1. **Read daily**—Reading the Bible every day gives you continual insight to know and choose God's will. *"But his delight is in the law of the Lord, and on his law he meditates day and night."* (Psalm 1:2)

2. **Study thoroughly**—Reflecting numerous times on a passage of scripture plants its counsel more deeply in your heart. *"I meditate on your precepts and consider your ways. ... Your statutes are my delight; they are my counselors."* (Psalm 119:15, 24)

3. **Memorize regularly**—Memorizing the Word of God strengthens resistance against temptations that could entice you away from God's purposes. *"I have hidden your word in my heart that I might not sin against you."* (Psalm 119:11)

4. **Inquire frequently**—Asking questions of spiritually mature Christians (especially a small group leader or pastor) provides safety as you interpret God's will from scripture. *"The way of a fool seems right to him, but a wise man listens to advice."* (Proverbs 12:15)

5. **Apply constantly**—Putting the Word of God into action reinforces its life-giving nature and transforming power to keep you in God's will. *"This has been my practice: I obey your precepts."* (Psalm 119:56) *"Therefore everyone who hears these words of mine and puts them into practice is like a wise man who built his house on the rock."* (Matthew 7:24)

Chapter 5
Discussion Questions

1. What is your response to the fact that only 18% of American Christians read the Bible daily?

2. In what area of Hebrews 6:1-2 do you have questions and need further instruction?

3. How have you observed the scheme of ignorance influencing society? The church?

4. Give an example of something you believed to be true, but discovered was false after reading scripture. How did your discovery change your attitude, perspective, or behavior?

5. On which of the 5 guidelines do you need to concentrate most?

Chapter 6

Imitation

"The whole conduct of life is based on this: that what we admire in others we want to do ourselves."
Quintillian

Our first child was very compliant. I can't recall spanking her because a firm word imme-diately corrected the slightest misbehavior. As a toddler, she played with Squeaky Bear. He was an ugly, white plastic bear, named Squeaky because of the irritating high-pitched noise he made when squeezed. I never enjoyed Squeaky Bear. In fact, I often stepped on him when I walked through a room in which he was left on the floor.

One day, passing through the living room, I gave Squeaky Bear a foot to the mid-section. He released a loud, piercing cry. Suddenly, our daughter came running in from her bedroom not knowing why he cried. She picked up her toy friend, comforted him with hugs and kisses, asking again and again,

"Squeaky Bear, are you ok?" She held him tightly until he supposedly calmed down.

As I watched her, something spiritual occurred to me, if you can believe it. She treated Squeaky Bear the same way I treated her! When she was hurt, in pain, stepped on, or simply crying, I would come at once. Then I'd lift her into my arms and console her until she re-gained composure. Now our little girl imitated me. She became like me by following my example.

The power of imitation is profound. It can change the way people live. So the Bible urges us, *"Be imitators of God, therefore, as dearly loved children and live a life of love, just as Christ loved us and gave Himself for us as a fragrant offering and sacrifice to God."* (Ephesians 5:1-2) Imitation is the most common form of learning and we learn most effectively in our spiritual maturation by imitating our Lord. He loved us dearly and sacrificially, so we love others like we've been loved.

Spiritual leaders offer examples to imitate as well. In the early church Paul served as apostle, evangelist, pastor and teacher. His lifestyle as a devoted disciple provided a model for all Christians to follow. As a humble servant of the Lord, he exhorted younger Christians to obey his public teachings and imitate his personal behavior: *"Whatever you have learned or received or heard from me, or seen in me—put it into practice..."* (Philippians 4:9)

The renowned John Wesley lived a life worth imitating. He preached the gospel, founded Methodism, and wrote religious literature in England during the 18th century. As his writings increased in popularity and sales, his income dramatically changed. At one point he was making the equivalent of $160,000 per year in today's money, however he remained on his longtime budget of $20,000 per year.[1] Therefore, he could and did give away $140,000 annually. Unlike most everyone, Wesley didn't increase his living expenses as his income climbed and climbed … a leader worth imitating.

The father heart of God and leaders characterizing His heart present two models, then, for spiritual imitation. We must make sure, of course, that our spiritual leaders—pastors, teachers, and mentors—truly imitate Christ themselves. Spurring Corinthian believers forward, Paul wrote, *"Follow my example, as I follow the example of Christ."* (1 Corinthians 11:1) His words remind us to exercise wisdom in choosing who we imitate. This is especially important for new Christians who prove most vulnerable in gravitating toward well-meaning leaders who do not live a balanced, Christ-centered life.

Some of these deficient leaders exhibit an ultra-conservatism characterized by man-made rules and regulations. On the other hand, some delight themselves by dancing in and out of appropriate spiritual boundaries at their own discretion. Interestingly, both groups major on minors. The first set emphasizes what Christians can't do and the second set underscores what Christians can do. One enforces rigidity while the other champions liberty. Balance is a delicate place.

To find that place we must turn to scripture and

specifically to Jesus. One day He was tested by an expert in the law, an ultra-conservative who adhered to rules. *"Teacher, which is the greatest commandment in the Law?" Jesus replied, "Love the Lord your God with all your heart and with all your soul and with all your mind. This is the first and greatest commandment. And the second is like it: Love your neighbor as yourself."* (Matthew 22:37-39) Christ majored on the majors as His ensuing words verify: *"All the Law and the Prophets hang on these two commandments."* (Matthew 22:40)

In other words, love is paramount! The love of Christ fulfills the Old Testament. Everything God was and is about centers on love. Jesus came from heaven to earth as the exact representation of the Father, deity in flesh, to preach this love. And He came to demonstrate perfect love in offering Himself as a sacrifice, the substitution for the penalty of our sins. He took death in our place. This is the place, then. This is where we discover the balanced life, one in which we refuse to yield under the unhealthy control of supposed leaders and ignore the dangerous license of would-be shepherds. Instead, we walk in the path of the cross, from which we were first loved. This is the locale of love, loving God in return and loving others as God loved us. We major on the majors like Jesus did. Imitation? Imitate God and only those who imitate God.

As seen, when we imitate those who fail to imitate the Lord we readily fall prey to either legalism or license. Let's look at legalism. Consider a church protesting the funeral of a young military man killed in action while serving our country. How could such an atrocity happen? How could a group professing the name of Jesus do this to the victim's family? The young soldier protected our national freedom from terrorism.

Nevertheless, these merciless demonstrations go on. Why? Extreme beliefs. Fanatical viewpoints of an illegitimate leader are adopted by others and then hateful displays paraded with rabid zeal. Wrongful imitation! The beliefs behind such malicious behaviors include the notion that God is releasing His wrath upon the United States through the deaths of American soldiers because of our society's acceptance of homosexuality. Here we have legalism, a self-righteous attitude that elevates personal opinion above biblical accountability and ruthlessly devalues others. The Bible clearly denounces homosexuality, but it is ludicrous to use the sin of same-sex behavior as the rationale for military deaths.

What about something maybe less reactionary? For instance, a pastor tells his congregation to read nothing but the Bible. On the surface it sounds good. But, is it? What's wrong with reading books? Biographies to learn about history and heroes, theology to learn about systematic thinking, psychology to learn about personalities and perceptions, bestsellers to learn about investing money and decreasing debt? And apart from reading newspapers and other media information we couldn't know the events of our world or understand how to relate to people in our world.

The Bible was written to reveal the nature of God.

It helps us in every aspect of life. However, the revelation of God's nature is not a textbook on science,
finances, history, sociology, parenting, psychology,
engineering, languages (not even Hebrew or Greek).
Therefore, don't imitate people who say naive and/
or controlling things like, "Only read the Bible." It's
just another form of legalism. Scripture remains the
inspired, inerrant, and infallible Word of God. At the
same time, to live as a culturally relevant person
with godly influence we must be aware of human
history, the present state of society, and the chal-
lenges of our shared future.

License is the other side of the coin. Legalism and
license, two broken paths of imitation. License even-
tuates when we copy the attitudes and actions of
those trying to prove their significance. For instance,
in recent years the emerging/emergent church
movement has garnered attention for its smooth
talking spokespersons and creative writers. Some
leaders in the movement, targeted at 18-30 year
olds, have developed huge churches and authored
best-sellers. It doesn't take long, however, for the
discerning reader of emerging/emergent church
literature to realize the reactive mentality underly-
ing their liberal notions of "repainting Christianity."

Why repaint Christianity? One over-arching
reason ... because these folks don't like the church
of recent generations, or at least parts that feel
too restrictive for their twenty-first century ideas.
The emerging/emergent objective to "embrace the
culture" certainly lines up with the Great Commission
wherein Jesus said, *"Go and make disciples of all*

nations..." (Matthew 28:19) However, their reactive nature toward biblical faith and practice has catapulted the movement beyond sound teaching. As advocates for drinking and swearing, for instance, they have forgotten the law of love. As ambiguous pertaining to homosexuality, they have enabled same-sex sin. As jugglers relevant to Christian doctrine, they have devalued the very Word of God.

Not all in this movement have wandered from allegiance to the straight-forward truth of scripture. Nevertheless, discernment here is especially warranted. Why? Because in the absence of discernment, embracing the culture quickly converts into absorbing the culture. And looking like the culture has always captured the cool factor. After all, when was it cool to be just a devoted Christ-follower? Therefore, personal significance is far too significant in the emerging/emergent church. It's an invitation of "come to Christ and be cool"! What a deal. You can turn from the kingdom of darkness to the kingdom of light and not necessarily deny your sin-bent self. No surprise this movement has integrated so many.

Imitating Jesus plus Culture appeals to human nature, i.e., "you can have (keep) your cake and eat it too." Not possible though. Jesus said, "*If anyone would come after me, he must deny himself and take up his cross daily and follow me. For whoever wants to save his life will lose it, but whoever loses his life for me will save it.*" (Luke 9:23-24) Deny self or serve self. Christ-centered or self-centered.

At the core of all self-centeredness lies pride,

sourced in its originator, Satan. Pride seduced Satan (initially an angel) to try to be like God. It wasn't humble imitation. His ambition epitomized selfishness. As a result, he was thrown out of heaven to roam the earth as God's enemy, tempting you and me to imitate ego-centric behaviors. "*How you have fallen from heaven, O morning star, son of the dawn! You have been cast down to the earth, you who once laid low the nations! You said in your heart, 'I will ascend to heaven; I will raise my throne above the stars of God; I will sit enthroned on the mount of assembly, on the utmost heights of the sacred mountain. I will ascend above the tops of the clouds; I will make myself like the Most High.' But you are brought down to the grave, to the depths of the pit.*" (Isaiah 14:12-15)

Satan was created by God and given an extremely distinguished position, but imitated God in an oppositional way: "*I will make myself like the Most High.*" In other words, he wanted to exalt himself to the level of God, not humble himself in his God-given responsibility. Thus, his dismissal from heaven.

Satan is a Hebrew word meaning adversary. A list of his names in the Bible includes adversary, devil, enemy, serpent, evil one, Beelzebub, prince/god of this world, and prince of the power of the air. He launches attacks against Christians to detract from godliness and against unbelievers to distract from the gospel. However, our enemy has not escaped God's sovereign rule over the universe. Therefore, he can only do what God permits.

Also realize that Satan cannot read minds and

know the future. Otherwise, the devil would be equal to God, contrary to what God says about Himself: *"I am God, and there is none like Me, declaring the end from the beginning and from ancient times things not yet done."* (Isaiah 46:9-10)

Imitation was the primary reason for the downfall of Satan in the beginning of creation and has remained one of his major ploys throughout history. For example, he utilized it during the Israelites trek in the wilderness: *"But they would not listen and were as stiff-necked as their fathers, who did not trust in the Lord their God. They rejected His decrees and the covenant ... They imitated the nations around them although the Lord had ordered them, 'Do not do as they do,' and they did the things the Lord had forbidden them to do."* (2 Kings 17:14-15) Contrary to God's command, the Hebrew nation bowed to the scheme of imitation and copied the culture around them. No wonder it took 40 years to complete an 11-day journey. *"God opposes the proud."* (James 4:7)

A New Testament corollary says, *"Do not conform any longer to the pattern of this world, but be transformed by the renewing of your mind."* (Romans 12:2) The mind is where the battle wages. It must be renewed by eliminating the misbelief that significance is found in being like others, and realizing we ultimately discover true purpose by imitating God as His dearly loved children.

Satan's scheme of imitation confronts us on every front imaginable. Take athletics for example. How much time, energy and money is spent on children in an effort to imitate athletic success, making our kid the next Albert Pujols, Roger Federer, Maria Sharapova, David Beckham, or Dwayne Wade? I know a couple who spent $30,000 in one year for private lessons and other tennis expenses for their two children. Neither child was an outstanding player regionally, let alone nationally. Tennis provides great exercise but this presses the question, "when is enough enough?"

The scheme of imitation certainly tempts us when it comes to wealth. A friend buys a new car and suddenly our car loses its appeal. We visit someone in their large new house and go home thinking of how we can put on an addition. Imitation of what others have readily produces distraction, discontentment and debt, buying what we want but don't need.

Imitation via peer pressure remains our enemy's most powerful weapon when it comes to teenagers. My wife and I raised 3 children. We cautioned them during their high school years with this proverb: *"He who walks with the wise grows wise, but a companion of fools suffers harm."* (Proverbs 13: 20) We knew the inherent power of relationships. We understood the effect a young person could have on another. Put simply, we become like those with whom we associate. Therefore, we wanted to ensure, as far as we could, that our children would forge healthy relationships, imitating godly people.

However, most don't, giving in to the pressure of friends to drink, view porn, take drugs, or engage in pre-marital sex. Also did you know the startling fact that almost 9 out of 10 church-attending high schoolers cease involvement in a church once they leave home?[2] Why? More than a singular reason. But clearly the influence of friends is at play. Concerning sex, almost all teens (94%) believe they should receive a message from society to abstain from sexual relations until at least after high school. But nearly 50% of 12-18 year olds feel pressure from friends to participate in sex.[3] Writing to the church in Corinth, which was highly vulnerable to sexual sin, the apostle Paul exclaimed, *"Bad company corrupts good character."* (1 Corinthians 15:33) Be careful, then, about relationships. We will, in all probability, become like those close to us.

Even inside the church the scheme of imitation can entrap us if we equate acceptance or success with certain people or particular ministries. "If I could just be like them!" "What if God let me do ministry like they do?" "How awesome if I had the spiritual gifts they have." Imitation, imitation, imitation. Don't go there! God longs for you to be who He made you to be, as scripture teaches, *"By the grace of God I am who I am."* (1 Corinthians 15:10) You are not supposed to look like whoever. Instead, you are to be who you are as you imitate God and imitate His character in people worth emulating.

Without question, imitation is two-sided. On the positive side, we imitate God as His dearly loved children and follow trustworthy leaders in the church. Hopefully family and friends also display Christ-like qualities. But we must be aware of the negative side, for the world in which we live contains countless examples which are bad examples. Satan yearns to put these before us as worthy of our time, energy and money. But they're not. They only disclose his clever scheme bent on wasting our time, depleting our energy, and stealing our money. God has a better plan. It starts and ends with imitating Him.

Chapter 6
Discussion Questions

1. Share a memory from your childhood of imitating a positive attitude or behavior.

2. What is a common lie lurking beneath the surface of Satan's scheme of imitation?

3. Are you primarily a leader or follower? How has that helped you, or not helped you, in imitating godly examples?

4. Have you ever been tempted in your Christian life to turn toward legalism? Toward license? What happened?

5. On a scale of 1 (low) to 10 (high), how satisfied are you with being who you are in Christ, uniquely you, not hoping to be someone else?

Chapter 7

Insecurity

"Great tranquility of heart is his who cares for neither praise nor blame."
Thomas à Kempis

*E*verybody feels insecure at times. A few years ago I heard Wayne Simien, All-American basketball player at Kansas University, as he described his own insecurity. He was haunted by anxiety about his performance on the court coupled with fear of criticism from sportswriters in the newspapers. But something changed. At the beginning of his junior year Wayne turned the control of his life over to Jesus Christ, ending his desperation for the accolades of men, beginning his journey for the applause of heaven. An audience of One. His spiritual turnaround made the difference. Insecurity lost its grip.

Simien's testimony helps define insecurity. It revolves around the desire to please people to the expense of pleasing God, worrying about our

performance while losing sight of God's prece-
dence. Insecurity, then, is misplaced trust. And trust
in a person or circumstance, instead of God, leaves
us conflicted. We long for human affirmation and
acceptance, but innately suspect it won't meet our
need. Still, apart from God, we strive to gain a sense
of security, a tranquility of heart divorced from the
need of praise and the fear of blame. Like Simien,
though, we must cease our futile efforts and humbly
receive the gracious gift only available by God's
grace, the love of Jesus. This is the only love that
satisfies, unconditional love.

Even spiritual heroes faced insecurity. Called by
God to deliver the nation of Israel from slavery in
Egypt, Moses questioned himself: *"Who am I, that
I should go to Pharaoh and bring the Israelites out
of Egypt?"* (Exodus 3:11) The Lord responded, *"I
will be with you..."* (Exodus 3:12) Moses looked to
his own ability, not God's omnipotence. No wonder
he felt distressed and deemed himself unqualified.
Misplaced trust.

Like Moses, so it was with Gideon. When
commissioned to end Midian's oppression of the
Israelites, Gideon replied: *"Did not the Lord bring
us out of Egypt? But now the Lord has abandoned
us and put us into the hand of Midian."* (Judges
6:13) He acknowledged the Jews miraculous escape
from Egypt. But Gideon no longer recognized God's
faithfulness, for the Midianite army had ravaged his
fellow-Hebrews for seven years, ruining the land and
impoverishing the people. God addressed Gideon as
a "mighty warrior," but Gideon was terrified. The

possibility of failure seemed overwhelming.

Aaron, the brother of Moses, succumbed to insecurity when he encountered resistance from the Israelites who waited impatiently for Moses to descend from Mount Sinai. As Moses met with God on the Mount to receive the commandments, people stubbornly insisted on something new to worship, saying, *"Come make us gods who will go before us. As for this fellow Moses who brought us up out of Egypt, we don't know what has happened to him."* (Exodus 32:1) Aaron, second in charge, identified with their panic. He made an idol. Did you ever think something had to happen because God wasn't accommodating our schedule? That something represents insecurity. Insecurity forgets that God's ways are not our ways, His timing is not our timing. Insecurity grasps for control.

Insecurity readily affects all ages. A pre-schooler jumps into the deep end of a pool because older kids urge him on. An adolescent runs across a dangerous highway because his friends dare him. A teenage girl gives away her virginity because her boyfriend threatens to break up with her if she refuses. A forty year old man watches porn with a friend out of fear of being labeled "holier than thou." Striving to please people can provoke insecurity into action, unwise at best, sometimes dangerous, and often sinful.

In the Old Testament, Saul serves as a glaring example of insecurity turned sinful. Although he maintained access to anything he wanted as King of Israel, Saul's self-esteem and confidence were shaken as he monitored the success of David, a young military hero: "*They have credited David with tens of thousands, he thought, but me with only thousands. What more can he get but the kingdom? And from that time on Saul kept a jealous eye on David.*" (1 Samuel 18:8-9)

Competitive jealousy fueled Saul's insecurity. He had to be the man. And if he couldn't be the man, then nobody could be the man. So he spent 14 years chasing David around the wilderness, trying to kill his perceived rival. David continually escaped the jealous rage of Saul and eventually replaced him as king. Doesn't that sound familiar? The very circumstance we fear, the one thing we seemingly must control, ends in self-sabotage. Insecurity loses.

From the above illustrations we surely resonate with the following description of insecurity from Joseph Nowinski: "Insecurity refers to a profound sense of self-doubt—a deep feeling of uncertainty about our basic worth and our place in the world. Insecurity is associated with chronic self-consciousness, along with a chronic lack of confidence in ourselves and anxiety about our relationships. The insecure man or woman lives in constant fear of rejection and a deep uncertainty about whether his or her own feelings and desires are legitimate."[1]

To summarize thus far, insecurity germinates in the soil of misplaced trust. Instead of focusing on God's faithfulness, this scheme fixates on the following:

- Individual ability - "Who am I?" - Moses
- Circumstantial fear - "The Lord has abandoned us." - Gideon

- Personal resistance - "Come, make us gods." - Aaron
- Competitive jealousy - "What more can he get but the kingdom?" - Saul

These are some of the major contexts in which insecurity shows up with its correlating misbeliefs, "Who am I?," "The Lord has abandoned us," etc. Some might believe the totality of Satan's lie ... that we are downright worthless. Fortunately, as with all the devil's schemes, the truth of scripture delivers us from living under the oppression of any and all misbeliefs.

The Bible declares truth with profound clarity: *"The Lord will be your confidence and will keep your foot from being snared."* (Proverbs 3:26) *"The man of integrity walks securely."* (Proverbs 10:9) *"His heart is steadfast, trusting in the Lord. His heart is secure, he will have no fear."* (Psalm 112:7-8) *"Trust in the Lord and do good; dwell in the land and enjoy safe pasture."* (Psalm 37:3) *"A righteous man may have many troubles, but the Lord delivers him from them all."* (Psalm 34:19)

One of my seasons of insecurity struck unexpectedly, when the church I founded grew far beyond my initial vision. Like Moses, I questioned myself, "Who am I? How can I lead such a big church? I'm not that strong of a pastor. My spiritual gifts aren't meant for a fellowship this size. I don't have what it takes!" Obviously, I took my eyes off Jesus. I needed an injection of truth. And Proverbs 3:26 was that truth: *"The Lord will be your confidence and will keep your foot from being snared."* That verse alone awakened a new level of trust in God as my strength. My spirit was unleashed to continue serving in the ministry entrusted to me, regardless of the size of the challenge. The scheme of Satan was averted and the devil's lies silenced, misbeliefs cast aside. And even more people reached for the kingdom of God. He is my security, yours too.

While walking through this time of insecurity, I discussed the subject with my wife. She reminded me of her many trips to Mississippi where our church rebuilt homes after the colossal damage of Hurricane Katrina. One house, different than all the others, was distinctively designed to withstand any hurricane winds, rain, and storm surge. This massive and expensive house, constructed primarily out of poured concrete, stood as a fortress defiant to any natural force. The exterior and interior walls appeared unmovable with rebar running through ton after ton of concrete for added strength and stability.

But then it happened. The hurricane-proof house took the brutal force of Katrina and disappeared. The only parts left were an underground garage, part of the foundational slab at ground level, and some twisted pieces of rebar sticking up where the exterior walls previously stood. A monumental lesson learned. The best we can do on our own will not withstand the storms that come our way. What we think is secure on earth is not.

Security is found only in one locale, the perfect love of Jesus Christ. His loving grace forgives all past sins when we realize our need of Him, confess our sinfulness to Him, and dedicate our life for Him. This is repentance, a spiritual turnaround in which we leave our self-centered, sinful life and start a Christ-centered, spiritual life. The Bible refers to this change as being born again. People often call it becoming a Christian, that is, an authentic follower of Christ.

As a disciple of Jesus we should deeply grasp how much we are loved, since we received His compassion demonstrated on the cross. He took our place, absorbing the penalty of our sins. He emancipated us from enslavement to sin and made us into new creations. We are servants of our Savior. He is Lord. We are secure in Him. Regrettably, issues from the past or present sometimes cloud our experience of divine love.

Lloyd Ogilvie tells of a pivotal point in understanding such love: "When I got good grades, achieved, and was a success, I felt acceptance from my parents. But, I rarely heard, 'Lloyd, I love you.' I felt empty."[2] This feeling carried over into his Christian life. While studying theology at the prestigious Edinburgh University in Scotland, he enrolled in a double load of classes. He writes, "I was exhausted by the constant feeling of never measuring up. Sadly, I was not living the very truths I was studying. Although I could tell you the Greek words for grace and joy I was not experiencing them."[3]

But then one day a favorite professor stopped Lloyd in a hallway. He describes the encounter: "He looked me in the eye intensely. Then he smiled warmly, took my coat lapels in his hands, and pulled me close to his face and said, 'Dear boy, you are loved now!'"[4] And so I say the same to anyone struggling with insecurity, "You are loved now!" Not when you improve, not when you achieve better grades, not when you work harder, not when you lose weight, not when you make more money, not when you buy a house, not when you are married, not when....

Satan schemes to keep you from delighting in God's love. He enjoys telling lies to draw your attention to what people might think and situations might require. Put an end to fear-based living. Place your trust in the Lord each day, each decision. You have nothing to prove. You are loved now!

Chapter 7
Discussion Questions

1. What are your thoughts about biblical heroes, like Moses, experiencing insecurity when they were called into ministry?

2. Do you believe everyone encounters insecurity? If so, why do you think insecurity is universal?

3. Insecurity occurs when we place our trust in someone or something other than God. Who or what represents your most susceptible area for misplaced trust? Examples: Money, Job, Ministry, Success, Family, Marriage, Popularity, Independence.

4. Tell about an experience in which you lacked confidence in the Lord?

5. Is there an issue from the past that clouds your experience of Christ's unconditional love? If so, explain.

Summary

Sometimes I don't read conclusions to books, figuring if I don't grasp the author's point by the end of the last chapter I won't get it by reading further. But let me urge you to read on. This summary will underscore the biblical prescription for resisting the schemes of Satan—his lies, misbeliefs, and temptations. And embracing the will of God—His truths, values, and purposes.

The primary biblical directive to rise above Satan's schemes is to put off the old self and put on the new self. The apostle Paul wrote to the Ephesian Christians, *"²²You were taught, with regard to your former way of life, to put off your old self, which is being corrupted by its deceitful desires, ²³to be made new in the attitude of your minds, ²⁴and to put on the new self, created to be like God in true righteousness and holiness."* (Ephesians 4:22-24) Paul knew what they were taught because he was their instructor, previously living in Ephesus for 3 years. During this period he spoke in their synagogue for 3 months, lectured daily in the Ephesian hall of Tyrannus for

2 years, and preached in their city amphitheatre which seated 25,000 people.

His message was simple, yet powerful. We choose at any moment necessary to put off the old self, the sinful nature, which governed our life before devotion to Christ. The old self is the part of us which still houses sinful desires and may be enticed to believe a misbelief and think a lie is truth. It remains receptive to temptation. Therefore, the sinful nature forms the target for Satan's schemes. Notice in verse 22 its desires are deceitful and lead only to spiritual corruption.

On the other hand, the new self is the divine nature of Jesus residing in us through the Holy Spirit, received at the point of our dedication to Christ. The new self directs our Christian life. It is the presence and power of Christ in us, enabling us to grow into the likeness of God in true righteousness and holiness (verse 24).

This maturation process evolves in our attitudes (verse 23), the ways we choose to think and believe. Opposing the sinful nature, the new self is the spiritual locale which welcomes the implantation of God's Word. Here He deposits truth, protecting us from the entrapments of Satan's schemes and motivating us toward the fulfillment of God's plans. The new self thinks and believes in agreement with scripture, armed for victory when the old self entertains devil-induced lies.

The apostle Paul continues to contrast the old self and new self by citing a few examples. *"25Therefore each of you must put off falsehood and speak truthfully to his neighbor, for we are all members of one body. [26]'In your anger do not sin': Do not let the sun go down while you are still angry, [27]and do not give the devil a foothold. [28]He who has been stealing must steal no longer, but must work, doing something useful with his own hands, that he may have something to share with those in need. [29]Do not let any unwholesome talk come out of your mouths, but only what is helpful for building others up according to their needs, that it may benefit those who listen."* (Ephesians 4:25-29) This paragraph can be organized as follows:

Old Self	New Self
(vs. 25) 1.Telling a lie	Telling the truth
(vs. 26) 2.Staying angry	Being angry
(vs. 28) 3.Stealing	Working
(vs. 29) 4.Unwholesome talk	Helpful talk

Right in the middle of these examples to put off the old and put on the new we read (verse 27), *"and do not give the devil a foothold."* Choosing to accept and act on a temptation opens the door for Satan to implement one of his schemes. Telling a lie, for instance, may appear harmless to the sinful nature. But it could easily start a pattern of taking after others who lack integrity, leading us down the dark road of deception and the scheme of imitation.

Spiritual warfare, then, usually boils down to the decisions we make. Do we believe a lie or believe the truth? Do we tell a lie or tell the truth? Do we feel angry and work through forgiving someone, or do we stay angry and let bitterness creep into our spirit?

I'll end this summary with two encouragements. First, temptation does not equal sin. Everyone faces temptation. And temptation surely points the way to sin. However, we must first buy into the lie presented to the mind of our sinful nature in order for temptation to escalate to the point of sin. We may be tempted to steal, for example. However, it's just a temptation. It morphs into sin only if we decide we will steal something. The external act of stealing, if it occurs, reveals that sin was already an internal choice.

Secondly, Satan possesses no automatic influence over anyone who follows Jesus Christ. The devil remains defeated since our Savior vanquished him on the cross, asserting the final verdict, *"It is finished!"* (John 19:30) C.S. Lewis describes Satan's power like that of an angry dog fiercely barking, but tied around a tree, unable to hurt us. Unless we decide to walk near and play with the malicious animal. Otherwise, we remain safe from harm. So it is with the father of lies. He strives to frighten us with the caustic barking of his temptations, but he is disempowered by the tree of Calvary. The devil can't touch us, unless we let him.

So rejoice! Give thanks for the new self Christ has formed in you. Put off the old self and its sinful possibilities by faithfully applying the Word of God to Satan's schemes. Freely rest in the loving arms of your heavenly Father as He continually transforms you from one degree of righteousness to another.

"Finally, brothers, whatever is true, whatever is noble, whatever is right, whatever is pure, whatever is lovely, whatever is admirable—if anything is excellent or praiseworthy—think about such things." (Philippians 4:8)

Endnotes

Chapter 1

1. Charisma Magazine, August 2006, p. 77,
   Alice Smith, "Tell Yourself the Truth."

Chapter 2

1. USA Today, June 23, 2006.
2. www.camphillcofc.org

Chapter 3

1. People Magazine, 7-20-09, p. 78.
2. Emons Barnett Technology & Digital
   Correspondent, July 2009.
3. NBC News, Nightline, 2-12-08.
4. Christianity Today, Jennifer Parker, "The Sex
   Lives of Christians," March/April 2003.
5. Christa.net
6. KC Star, Feb 23, 2006, B8.
7. C.S. Lewis, The New Encyclopedia of Christian

Quotations, Baker Books, 2000, Grand Rapids, Michigan, p. 298.

Chapter 4

1. Grace Awakening, Chuck Swindoll, Word Publishing, Dallas, 1990.

Chapter 5

1. Josh Billings, 19th Century humorist, source unknown.
2. "Behold the What?" Charles Swindoll, Orlando Conference, 1992.
3. Baptist Standard, 12-4-96, p. 1.
4. Barna.org, View on Spiritual Beings.
5. Christianity Today, Spring 2009, R7-R9, Sam Oneal. "American Christians and Bible Reading."
6. Christianity Today, September 12, 1977, p. 19.
7. Christian Healthcare Newsletter, September 2006, p. 10.
8. Beggaring Belief, David Yount, September 4, 2000, Scripps Howard News Service.

Chapter 6

1. Radical, David Platt, Multnomah Books, Colorado Springs, 2010, p. 126.
2. Southern Baptist Council on Family Life in Ministry ToolBox, 10-23-2002.

3. Pure Hope Publication citing Family Research Council statistics.

Chapter 7

1. Joseph Nowinski, The Tender Heart: Conquering Your Insecurity, New York, Friends Publishing, 2001, p. 23.
2. Lloyd Ogilvie, Enjoying God, Word Books, 1989.
3. Ibid.
4. Ibid.

CPSIA information can be obtained at www.ICGtesting.com
Printed in the USA
LVOW102044120712

289705LV00003B/2/P

9 781619 969063